FOR YOU,
YES, YOU. SERIOUSLY,
YOU! QUIT LOOKING
AROUND! IT'S FOR YOU!

Donna
&
Len

Oct 2016

Happy Halloween

3

4

5

7

9

10

12

14

17

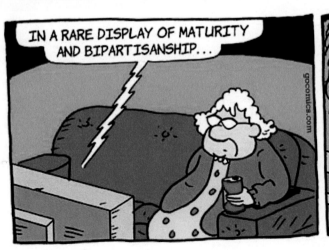

20

21

24

25

26

27

29

30

31

32

33

BZZZZZZ

BZZZZZZZZ

SWAT!

Living in harmony with nature.

LET'S GRAB A COFFEE.

I DON'T LIKE YOUR PLACE.

THE SILVER SPOON

THEY'RE SO SNOOTY ABOUT HOW YOU ORDER.

OH, PLEASE. THEY ARE NOT.

STEP UP, MOTHER. YOU'RE NEXT.

PREPARE TO BE MOCKED.

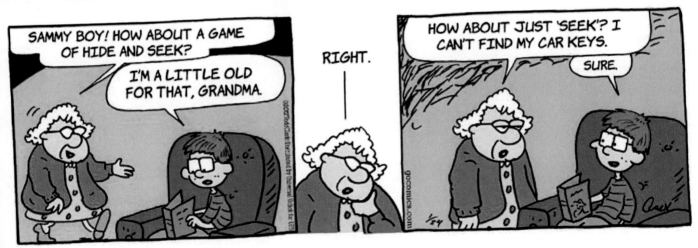

35

36

37

38

3/25

39

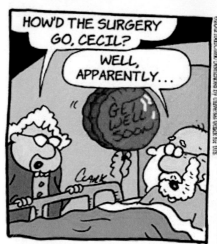

42

43

44

47

COULD YOU GO BRIGHTEN SOMEONE ELSE'S DAY FOR A WHILE?!

4/21

CAROL, THAT CHIHUAHUA IS ONE WEIRD-LOOKING CRITTER. HE FREAKS ME OUT.

YOU JUST NEED TO GET TO KNOW HIM BETTER.

WHEN THE MOTHERSHIP COMES, SPEAK KINDLY OF ME.

5/8

49

MRS. TRUMBO, I COULDN'T HELP BUT NOTICE YOU LOOK EXTRA SLIM LATELY.

MONTY, SUCKING UP UP TO THE TEACHER THE LAST WEEK OF SCHOOL WON'T HELP GRADES.

NOW, DID YOU ACTUALLY HAVE A QUESTION?

DID YOUR VOICE RECENTLY BECOME EVEN MORE ANGELIC?

MOVING ON...

I GOT IT! I GOT IT!

BONK!

www.killer-excuses.com

51

57

58

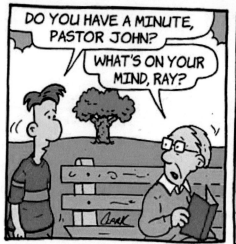

63

65

69

70

73

74

MY VIDEO SELF AND MY REALITY SELF ARE WORLDS APART.

MOTHER. YOU NEED TO WIPE OFF YOUR GLASSES BEFORE THE NEXT PLAY.

WHAT DO YOU MEAN?! THAT WAS A PERFECT TOUCHDOWN PASS!

YES...

BUT WHAT YOU THREW ME WAS THE GLYNN FAMILY'S CHIHUAHUA. THAT SCORE DOESN'T COUNT.

LOLA, I DON'T THINK WE SHOULD PLAY WORDS WITH FRIENDS ANYMORE.

WHY NOT, ETTA?

WE'RE TOO COMPETITIVE WITH EACH OTHER. IT'S NOT HEALTHY.

NONSENSE.

YEAH? SINCE I WON THAT MOST RECENT GAME...

YOUR LAST THREE WORDS HAVE BEEN "JERK", "MEANIE" AND "CHEATER."

PURE COINCIDENCE.

EVERYONE, THIS IS JERRY FROM LOWE'S.

WHAT'S THAT ALL ABOUT?

USUALLY ON ABOUT RAY'S EIGHTH TRIP BACK TO THE STORE...

THE GUYS FIGURE IT'S QUICKER IF THEY JUST COME FINISH HIS PROJECT.

79

80

82

87

88

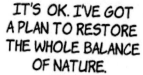

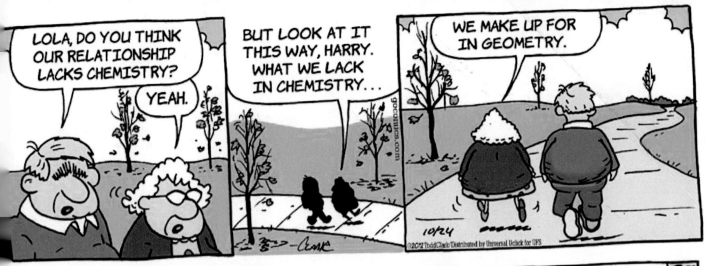

97

ETTA IT'S NO SECRET YOU AND I ARE VERY COMPETITIVE WITH EACH OTHER.

SENIOR CENTER

BUT I MUST SAY, YOU'RE ALWAYS A GRACIOUS WINNER.

THANKS. PROBABLY BECAUSE I GET SO MUCH PRACTICE.

HEY!!

WHAT ARE THESE THINGS, SAMMY?

GRANDMA SAYS THEY'RE "PAY PHONES."

PEOPLE WOULD PUT MONEY IN THEM AND MAKE A CALL.

AND WHY WERE THEY ATTACHED TO STRIPPER POLES?

DIFFERENT TIMES, MONTY. DIFFERENT TIMES.

99

100

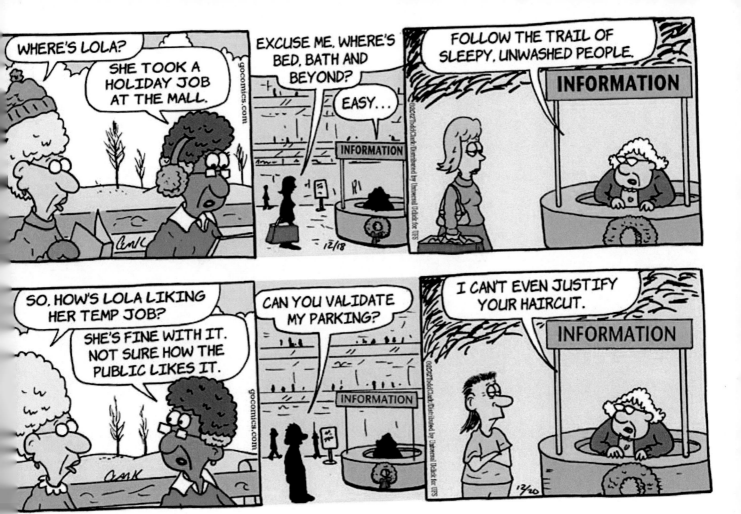

TODD AND LOLA ENJOY A LIGHT-HEARTED, NON-PHOTOSHOPPED MOMENT TOGETHER.

36304350R10061

Made in the USA
Middletown, DE
29 October 2016